The Power of Our Thinking!

Living from your authentic power

Alex Peeters & Marleen Devisch

Author: **Marleen Devisch**
Co-author: **Alex Peeters**
Cover design & composer: **Alex Peeters**
ISBN: **979-83-2722-800-9** (paperback)
Publisher: GROEI ACADEMIE BV
Press-work: **Amazon**
Edition: **2ᵉ print**
© 2024-2026 GROEI ACADEMIE BV, **Marleen Devisch** & **Alex Peeters**

All rights reserved by Alex Peeters & **Marleen Devisch,** GROEI ACADEMIE BV. No part of this publication may be reproduced and/or made public by means of print, photocopy, microfilm, internet or in any other way and/or by any medium without permission of both authors! You may not ask for/earn money based on this work without permission from both authors!

We have done our best to be as accurate and clear as possible. How you interpret the information offered is your responsibility.

Should you find errors in this book of any kind, please provide us with your feedback. Some of what we have written down here we have learned, read, unconsciously absorbed, borrowed or copied ourselves from someone else who is much smarter than us and/or who in turn has also learned it from others. No one needs to reinvent the wheel to be successful. We can embellish that wheel, imitate it, give it status, add our own input to it. That's called 'innovating'. Innovating is the most powerful way to be successful and to grow as human beings and as a human species.

https://groeiacademie.be

Inhoudsopgave

- Word of thanks 5
- About the authors 7
- Foreword 9
- Introduction 13
- What is thinking? 15
- We think in pictures 17
- Consciousness vs. Subconscious Mind 19
  - Consciousness 19
  - Subconscious 20
- The power of your thoughts 25
- Our intellectual muscles 27
  - What are those intellectual muscles? 27
    - Intuition 27
    - Imagination 28
    - Memory 29
    - Perception 30
    - Reason 30
    - Will 31
- Communication models 33
  - Stickperson 34
    - The Conscious mind (thinking) 35
    - The Subconscious mind (feeling, is actually the past) 35
    - Body (feelings, actions, and results, serving your mind) 36
  - NLP Communication Model 37
    - External event 37
    - Filters 38
    - Internal representation 40
    - Mood/State of mind 40
    - Body position 40
    - Behavior 41
    - Results 41
    - Our filters work in two directions 45
- The Barriers of Fear, ... 55
- the Terror Barrier 55
  - How does sabotage work? 56
  - Vicious Sabotage Circle 57
    - Forgiveness 58
    - Stop Judging 59
  - Break through the 'Barrier of Fear, ... 61
  - the Terror Barrier' 61
    - Would you like to get out of your comfort zone? 61

Afterword	73
References	75
Books	75
Audiobooks	78
GROEI ACADEMIE	79
The Society of NLP	80

Word of thanks

I, Alex Peeters, would like to thank all the people who contributed directly or indirectly to the production of this book. I would like to take this opportunity to thank them for their support, commitment, and trust.

First and foremost, I would like to thank Marleen, because without her, I would never have completed this adventure.

In addition, I would like to thank my soul mates for their inexhaustible patience. Without their moral support, the realization of this book would not have been possible.

Finally, I also want to thank all my proofreaders, reviewers, friends, acquaintances, customers... for the support, their input, and/or the listening ear they have offered me.

I, Marleen Devisch, am grateful that I could contribute to this book. Alex has laid the foundations for it. I have added my own experience to it.

That experience has come about through the many conversations I have had over the past 25 years with people who came to ask for my help. They have always been great gifts that accelerated my growth.

This book was made possible thanks to the synergy between two people. It has been a very enriching experience to embark on this adventure together with Alex. One plus one is much more than two!

In turn, I am grateful to all those who have contributed directly or indirectly to this book. With every input, a little stone has been moved that has brought us to this result.

About the authors

Marleen & Alex help people change their lives so that they spend more time feeling good than feeling bad. In short, they help people on their way to maximum quality of life, happiness and success.

We build our own prison of thought. Only to be unhappy because we think that way. We twist ourselves into it. This causes great unfreedom in our lives.

Marleen & Alex work with NLP (Neuro-Linguistic Programming) so that they can gently move towards a life where other thoughts and feelings come to the foreground. More freedom, joy and impact are the result and so is a different way of life.

Alex Peeters & Marleen Devisch

Marleen & Alex have been business partners in addition to life partners since October 2013. They are both directors of GROEI *ACADEMIE BV*

Marleen Devisch, NLP Trainer™, NLP Coaching Trainer™, NLP Coach™ and mentor at GROEI **ACADEMIE**, life partner of Alex, has been active within personal development for over a quarter of a century. She understands the art of creating a climate of growth for people. Her great all-round experience with and understanding of people, makes her an indispensable supporter for anyone who follows training. She specializes in getting people in touch with the core of their personality and with their inner motivators. The calmness and simplicity of her approach and her enthusiasm are very inspiring and get people moving.

Alex Peeters, NLP Trainer™, NLP Coaching Trainer™, NLP Coach™ and mentor at GROEI *ACADEMIE, is the textbook example of what transformation someone at* GROEI *ACADEMIE can go through. Several years ago, he was diagnosed with autism. Hardly anyone believed he could become a trainer. Now he is an expert in business NLP training. He puts his autism to full use as a strength, so with his precision and sharp observations, he lifts people to an above-average level in their growth process. At* GROEI *ACADEMIE, he is the creator of many trainings. He is behind most of the books published by* GROEI *ACADEMIE. His passion for human growth is contagious.*

Foreword

Several years ago I met my husband. When the phase had come to allow me to look in the cupboards at his home, I found a treasure trove of elaborated texts. I discovered that he had a habit of writing things for himself, so thoroughly that it was almost a finished book. And then he lost interest in his writings, and they ended up on the shelf, while he was already working on a new theme.

I then kicked him in the ass, and we started publishing some of his written documents. You hold one of the first books we published.

And when the first edition was published, we were still looking for all kinds of ways that could help people in their growth process. We wanted to offer them an overview of possibilities, methodologies, and routes they could follow and explore to promote their personal development.

And we have also followed these paths ourselves. In the end, we were left with two roads, namely NLP (Neuro-Linguistic Programming) and RMP (Reiss Motivation Profile). And it has become our main avenue to help people. In our way of thinking, everything we have explored is somehow embedded in NLP & RMP. And we have left the other roads behind us and chose to become thoroughly proficient in two things.

And we could have taken this book off the circuit because a lot of things in it have become obsolete for us in the meantime. However, we have chosen to continue publishing this. Because every growth path we explore can be an eye-opener for someone. Everyone has to decide their growth paths in life. There are many possibilities, and we want to continue to encourage people to explore these possibilities.

We also want to encourage people to choose after an exploration time. Choose a direction, a method that suits you and that you feel comfortable with. Go down that road. Don't get stuck on a ten-lane highway. There is a great chance that you will pick up something from a great many things but always get stuck in a superficial layer of them. Personal development is a thorough process and this requires choices, commitment, focus, investment in time, money, and energy.

We are curious where this book will lead you. We wish you a very beautiful and exciting growth path. Your comments and questions are always welcome. You can reach us via https://www.groeiacademie.be/

> "The sculpture is already complete within the marble block before I start my work.
> It is already there, I just have to chisel away the superfluous material."
> ~ Michelangelo

Are you ready to show who you are? Here we go!

Thank you for trusting us to embark on this journey with us!

Alex Peeters & Marleen Devisch

Licensed Trainers of Neuro-Linguistic Programming®

Licensed Coaching Trainers of Neuro-Linguistic Programming®

Introduction

Everyone thinks, in one way or another!

- But what exactly is thinking?
- Are we aware of what a powerful tool it is and how strongly it affects our lives?
- Are we sufficiently aware of how our thinking works and how we can adjust it?

Our thinking plays a crucial role in our growth process. If we learn to handle it properly, it becomes a sublime tool that works for us. We can control our thoughts to a great extent.

Have you become curious?

What is thinking?

We all think, all day long!

And the question is: 'does our way of thinking help us move forward?'

- Is it constructive?
- Is it leading somewhere?
- Will it help us to grow?
- Do we dare to be creative and allow new ideas?
- Or are we only guided by old habits?

When you want to grow, learning to think creatively, is a very important step to take!

> "We can't solve problems
> by using the same kind of thinking
> we used when we created them."
> ~ Albert Einstein

Only a few people consider their thinking!

It all seems quite complex and abstract. But is it?

We think in pictures

With our thinking, we can create images!

We can think of our garden and most people picture their garden at that moment. And we can think of a nice birthday party from a few years back, and we usually see some kind of 'internal DVD' playing on in our heads. And we can also think of a party that has yet to come and even then we often see an image.

And we are already forming images of what is to come, of what is not yet there. So we're able to think creatively about what's to come. And this is a phenomenal ability!

We can also play with these images. We can make them stand still or move. And we can make them bigger or smaller. And we can look at it as an outsider, or we can act ourselves in our 'movie', and much more...

Consciousness vs. Subconscious Mind

Consciousness

'Consciousness' is the awareness of what we hear, see, feel, smell & taste, through our five senses.

It is awareness of yourself as a person and of your surroundings. And it means you are able to reflect on yourself. And your consciousness contains your five senses, your conscious thoughts, and feelings.

------------------------------ **sea-level** ------------------------------

Subconscious

Our subconscious contains all processes that we are not aware of: 'we are not aware of all the possibilities we have within us'.

There are feelings that we are not aware of. And there are processes in our body that we don't know about. So, not all our thoughts are conscious.

And there are 'forgotten' memories and experiences in us. Our subconscious mind is a storage space for memories and experiences. New information entering our subconscious mind is linked to those previously stored experiences and memories. And that brings certain reactions and accompanying emotions with it.

Someone who has experienced many times in his life that he has not been taken into account may be hypersensitive if someone passes him in a store full of waiting customers. Standing in the store, noticing that someone passes you, ends up in your subconscious and links itself there with previous experiences. And that sets the charge of those previous experiences in motion. And we may get an overreaction in the here and now.

Our subconscious mind can also serve as a protection against painful experiences. We have 'forgotten' them. We unconsciously build in mechanisms and defense systems that protect us against real or perceived threats. And the defenses we often feel when new challenges or changes come our way comes from those defense mechanisms.

At birth, our subconscious mind is a blank slate. Initially, it is our environment that describes this sheet. The beliefs and reactions that our environment gives us in our early childhood are very strongly rooted in our subconscious. It molds very strongly our way of being, our behavior. It is our starting point for most of the choices we make in our lives. And it strengthens our own identity or slows it down.

> "The healthier your thoughts,
> the healthier the thoughts
> you plant in your children's heads."
> ~ Marleen Devisch

We are born with a 'blank sheet'. Unwritten. We are completely dependent on our surroundings. And this environment sows thoughts, beliefs, norms, and values in us. Our 'blank sheet' is initially described by our parents and educators, the school, friends, and so on. And thoughts are planted in us that help us grow. Also, beliefs and thoughts are implanted in us that goes against our nature.

A child who is entrepreneurial by nature and grows up with parents who have 'no risks' as their core value will find it more difficult to be entrepreneurial than an enterprising child who grows up with parents who are also entrepreneurial themselves and have no problem with that. And, as already indicated above, we take in everything that our environment tells and experiences as correct and true.

A small child has not yet built up enough internal strength and insight to filter out which influences it can let in and which it must let go of if it wants to be happy. And a small child is not yet able to cope with the beliefs of his environment.

So a child also takes in the beliefs that are limiting and that inhibit his growth. And it draws conclusions based on what it naturally feels and what its surroundings say about it. And the enterprising child in our example above will eventually associate 'being entrepreneurial' with a feeling of fear, as with every step it may need to hear: 'watch out!', 'caution', 'don't'...

And it will start to bend its natural reflexes because it has concluded that this is not okay.

Around puberty, we usually begin to question the beliefs of our environment. The awareness then gradually grows that we want certain things differently, that certain beliefs that we have been taught do not correspond with who we are and with what we want. And that awareness is necessary to set a process in motion and to be able to actively steer this growth process in the direction we want.

Your mind shows how your thoughts are made up of both conscious and subconscious thoughts and that your body is the instrument for taking the required actions.

Your thinking determines to a large extent how you feel. How you feel colors your behavior. And your behavior has a significant influence on the responses you get, on the results you get in your life. And this in turn determines your thinking.

If you want changes in what is happening in your life, you will first have to take a closer look at your thinking and feeling. Each of us thinks in a certain way. The way you currently think is the result of years of development of your beliefs. And some of those beliefs help us be ourselves, others hold us back and prevent us from achieving our big goals, our big dreams, and wishes, and desires.

And so these limitations in your life are limitations in your thinking!

The power of your thoughts

Our subconscious contains elements that have become, as it were, 'motorways' in our brain.

Thoughts, feelings, experiences that have been installed since childhood and which are therefore deeply rooted in us and have become second nature. And when these thought patterns hinder, slow down or block our growth, it is important that we become aware of them and that we learn to bend these patterns.

When you continue to hold on to old thought patterns, you continue to feed and act on the same thoughts. And you keep spinning in the same circle of thinking-feeling-doing.

You can break that cycle when you allow new thoughts. And gradually your feelings and behavior will also change, which will strengthen your new thinking patterns. And in this way, you gradually build up a new 'thought circle' and a new appearance.

So don't persist in anger, don't dwell in sadness or any difficult emotion. It's food for what you don't want.

There are many methods for letting in new thoughts. Visualizations and affirmations are two of them.

Our intellectual muscles

We are all familiar with muscles. We use them all day long. And we feel them when we've walked just a little too far when we stretch them. And we can train them and make them stronger and more flexible.

Our mind also has 'muscles', that is to say, intellectual muscles. And we can also start exercising and training these muscles.

They can be a tremendously valuable tool to help us achieve our goals!

By actively and consciously learning to use your intellectual muscles, your growth process can run much more efficiently, and it can also accelerate considerably. And the quality of our results is much higher when we use these muscles to the fullest potential.

What are those intellectual muscles?

Intuition
Intuition is our internal voice, free of noise, with which we can learn to connect. It is a connection with our

deepest being. When we make that connection, we have very quick access to our deep thoughts, our sense of what we want and don't want, of what we should and shouldn't do. Intuition is our internal compass. And when we follow our intuition, there is a good chance that our actions are the right ones.

Training this mental muscle means that we learn to trust it, that we learn to listen to it, that we learn to live from this power. It means that we learn to believe that our intuition never lies.

Our intuition is a deep sense from our subconscious mind. And we often disprove it with our logical mind.

Our intuition also helps us to pick up on the surrounding energy. Our intuition does not deceive us. And we can build on it.

Imagination
Imagination is the capacity to think consciously in images, to consciously create images about something we want to achieve. Crazy dreams. Small or big dreams. Our imagination is much greater than we suspect at

first sight. And we have trained this 'muscle' many times.

As kids, we could do it like the best. We have also learned to associate 'actively using our imagination' with something childish. Use your imagination and build images in your mind of what you want to do in your life and then do it.

> "If you can dream it, you can do it."
> ~ Walt Disney

Believing in what you want to achieve strengthens your imagination. And the more you believe in your dreams, the more likely you will turn them into action.

Memory

All our thoughts are stored in our memory. And not only our thoughts but also all the emotions that sometimes attach to them. The higher the emotional charge, the deeper certain things are rooted in our memory. And there are numerous techniques for training your memory.

Perception

You can look at everything from different angles. There is a front and a back to everything. And you can see everything from up close or far, from below or from above.

And everything that we know in our world is through our perception. Our perception gives us, on the one hand, the ability to see and, on the other, the ability to solve problems. And we are capable of altering our perception.

We can learn to look at things differently. Depending on how you look at something, your thoughts, and feelings about it may change. And that can produce new results.

Actively learning to play with this mental muscle can help you very much. And it prevents us from getting stuck in thoughts and emotions that are not moving us forward.

Reason

This is what you think. You can bring thoughts together to form ideas. And you can question ideas and convert them into concrete steps.

Often we make the mistake of reasoning before we have allowed ourselves to give our dream and our intuition full space.

We get a flash of intuition inside our consciousness and boom: '**immediately we reason it to pieces:**'
- How can that be?
- That's impossible?
- That's not realistic?

and so on.

In this way, we do not make choices based on our intuition, but based on our reasoning ability. It should be the other way around. And initially, you make choices with your intuition, because this intuition is the direct connection with your higher consciousness, with your deepest being as a human being.

Will

To achieve a goal, you need willpower.

You must focus on your goal and learn to persevere. You need to be able to gather the necessary energy, day after day, to take steps towards where you want to go.

And you require the discipline not to take every tempting side road you come across, but to stay on your chosen path. You require the strength to get up again after falling. And you require your free will to choose every day to walk the path that you want to walk.

Wallace D. Wattles, the author of 'The Science of Getting Rich' and 'The Science of Being Great', talks about your mental senses: perception, imagination, memory, reason, will, and intuition.

Napoleon Hill, the author of 'Think and Grow Rich', talks about the six intellectual faculties: perception, imagination, memory, reason, will, and intuition.

Source: 'The Science of Getting Rich' – Wallace D. Wattles, 1910
'The Science of Being Great' – Wallace D. Wattles, 1911
'Think and Grow Rich!' - Napoleon Hill, 1938

Communication models

We learned above how thoughts work in us and how we can use our intellectual muscles to amplify those thoughts and direct them in the direction that helps us grow.

And it will have become clear to you that we have systems in us that can facilitate or complicate this process.

But how do these systems work?

There are many models that explain this to us, here we discuss two:
- Stickperson
- NLP Communication Model

Stickperson

The stickperson was designed by Dr. Thurman Fleet. He makes a distinction between the conscious and the unconscious part of the human mind. In its design, the human mind is guiding, and the body reacts to what goes on in the mind. Information enters our minds through our senses. There it is transformed into images. And through all kinds of processes between consciousness and subconscious, these images are filtered and the information colored.

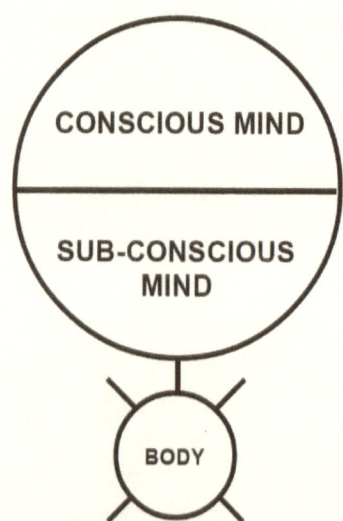

This model of the mind and body was originated by the late Dr. Thurman Fleet of San Antonio, Texas, [circa] 1934.

The Conscious mind (thinking)

This is the rational part of our mind. It is this part of us that makes choices, that builds reasoning. This part of us likes logic. The path our consciousness takes is strongly influenced by what we believe about ourselves, others, and the world. And the better we train our intellectual muscles, the better we can think with our consciousness in harmony with who we are.

> "We can't solve problems
> with the same thinking
> we used when we created them."
> ~ Albert Einstein

The Subconscious mind (feeling, is actually the past)

In the vision of Dr. Thruman Fleet, our subconscious mind is the real driving force of the human mind. It is in our subconscious mind that thoughts are linked to feelings. And it is there where beliefs are linked together to form complete systems of thoughts, feelings, and emotions that guide our behavior.

And our subconscious mind executes, from the information it has within it and from what it takes in through our conscious mind. From our consciousness, we can learn to feed, weaken, bend, disprove certain thoughts, and so on. And in this sense, our belief systems can be 're-educated' and brought more and more into line with who we are by nature.

Body (feelings, actions, and results, serving your mind) We need our bodies to take action. When we follow the logic of the Stickperson further, our body is an instrument that carries out what goes on in our conscious and subconscious minds. It is also through our body that others perceive our radiance. And our appearance is strongly influenced by all the thoughts and feelings that are going on in our conscious and subconscious minds at a particular moment.

Make sure that all 'Three Parts Work Together in Harmony' with each other!

NLP Communication Model

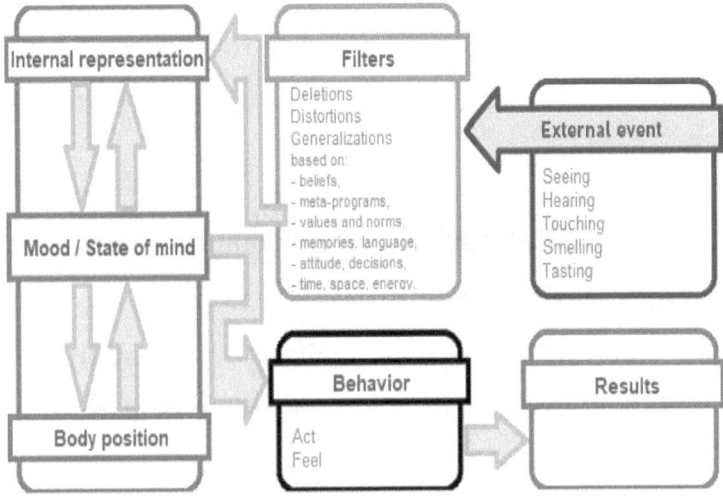

NLP Communication Model

The NLP Communication Model is the process from observation to behavior.

External event
Throughout the day we perceive the outside world through our five senses (seeing, hearing, touching, smelling, and tasting) and information stimuli are sent to us.

- What will happen to that?
- Where does this end up in our minds?
- What do we do with it in the end?

Filters

We take in an infinite amount of chaos of information. If we were to consciously perceive this, we would become overwhelmed. And for this reason, we filter all this information.

And we do this by subconsciously omitting, distorting, and generalizing things.

- **deletions**: without omitting information you feel overloaded with impressions that you consciously cannot handle to process,
- **distortions**: we speak of distortion when you base your current experience on a misrepresentation of your sensory impressions,
- **generalizations**: this means that you will draw global conclusions based on a few events, which you will subsequently accept as true.

We filter all information that comes to us based on our beliefs, our meta-programs (thinking styles from which you act and react), our values & norms, our memories, our language skills, our attitude, our decisions, our understanding of time, space, and energy.

For example, a friend tells you about his new dog. He enthusiastically describes his dog. Based on what you know about dogs, your experience with dogs, you will sort out what you hear, see, feel... If you like dogs and know a lot about them, you'll sort out differently than if you've been bitten by a dog before, if you're not an animal lover, and so on. You either want to find out more or you just don't. And you are going to take over the enthusiasm of the other person or just feel an aversion.

Our Subconscious Filters:
- beliefs,
- meta-programs,
- values and norms,
- memories,
- attitude,
- language skills,
- decisions,
- understanding of time, space, and energy.

Internal representation

After those stimuli have passed through your filtering system, you form an internal representation based on your external event and filter its information. And this internal representation is made up of images, sounds, feelings, smells, tastes, and our internal dialog.

Mood/State of mind

The internal representation and the body posture have an important interaction with each other. This creates the mood/state of mind and this ultimately guides your behavior and your result. In our example, you are creating an image of your friend's dog. And this image puts you in a certain state of mind.

Body position

That state of mind will be reflected in your posture: 'you smile, you move, you shrink back, and so on'. Your image, how you feel about it, and your posture are constantly interacting with each other. And the one amplifies the other.

Behavior

Your body pushes you into action. You are going to react to your friend in a certain way. Depending on how you feel, the response will be different. Perhaps you ask your friend to show you that dog as soon as possible. And you might shut up and think: 'Wow, how am I supposed to visit that friend when that darn dog is walking around there all the time!'

Results

Your friend will, of course, respond to this comment as well. And your response will therefore have a certain result. In our example, the result might affect the friendship.

This is how it always goes:
- external stimuli entering our senses,
- based on what's inside us in beliefs, memories..., we're going to filter those stimuli,
- based on those filtered stimuli, we form an image,
- and this image affects how we feel and on our body and vice versa,
- and from there, we will take action, respond,

- and these reactions give a certain result.

The NLP Communication Model tells us more about this:
- information enters our brain through our senses,
- and this information is filtered there, through deletions, distortions, and generalizations,
- and these **filters** are strongly influenced by, among other things:
  - our **beliefs**, that which is true or false for us, right or wrong,
  - our **values**, things that are of great importance to us and which are shaped by strong clusters of beliefs,
  - our **meta-programs**, from where we act. Everyone has all meta-programs. We just use them differently and not always growth-promoting. Some examples of meta-programs:
    - away from or towards,
    - similarities or differences,
    - global or detail.

- the filtered information 'lands' in a pool of already processed and stored information in our brain. It activates certain parts of it, and it connects with it,
- the result is that we make an '**internal representation**' of this event. We use different representation systems for this: '**visual, auditory, kinesthetic, olfactory & gustatory**'. And these representation systems consist of building blocks:
    - the **great building** blocks are **our senses**. We also call them '**main modalities**',
    - main modalities consist of **smaller building blocks**, called **submodalities**. And these determine the size, shape, color, intensity... of our internal representation.
- and this internal representation strongly determines the **chemistry of our brains** and consequently our **mood/state of mind**,
- and our state of mind (which is also expressed in our body) influences our **behavior**,

- and behavior is what is visible to others: 'our **outcome**',
- and that outcome, in turn, influences the **response of others**,
- and these responses are the input that we take in through our **five senses**,
- and then the circle starts again.

The 'communication circles' that we create in our heads in this way can help us or hinder or even block us.

NLP intervenes at the level of our internal representations and everything that makes these representations come about.

This changes our state of mind and everything that follows. If you look at most methods that can help people from this point of view, NLP is the absolute outsider. NLP does not work with the content of an experience, but with how it is stored in our brain. If you change how it is stored in your brain, you get a new way to deal with the same experience, a new way to live it. And NLP is a fast and in-depth way to shift our perspective on any issue.

Our filters work in two directions

On the one hand, we filter the information that comes to us from the outside. On the other hand, we also filter the information that we publish ourselves. What we want to say (**the depth structure**) and what we say (**the surface structure**) rarely run parallel to each other. Consequently, we are not congruent.

Within NLP there is a way to bring depth and surface structure closer to each other. Depth and surface structure have to do with **language patterns**. And those language patterns are contained in certain models.

The model that is used within NLP to surface unspoken information and to make what someone is saying more clear is the **Meta Model**. In the Meta Model, you will find all the filters we mentioned earlier. With each filter, you will see certain language patterns, which you can then break with specific questions. These questions contribute to increasing the congruence between what we want to say and what we communicate. And the Meta Model makes an abstract, vague language more concrete.

Below is a schematic overview of the different language patterns of the Meta Model:

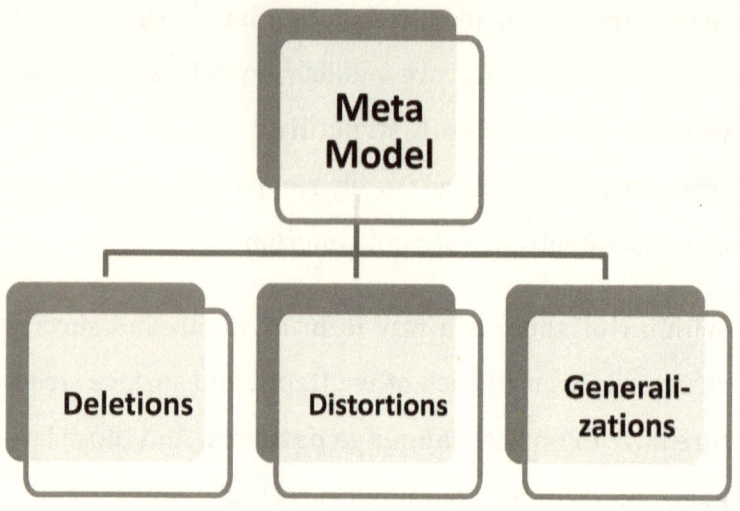

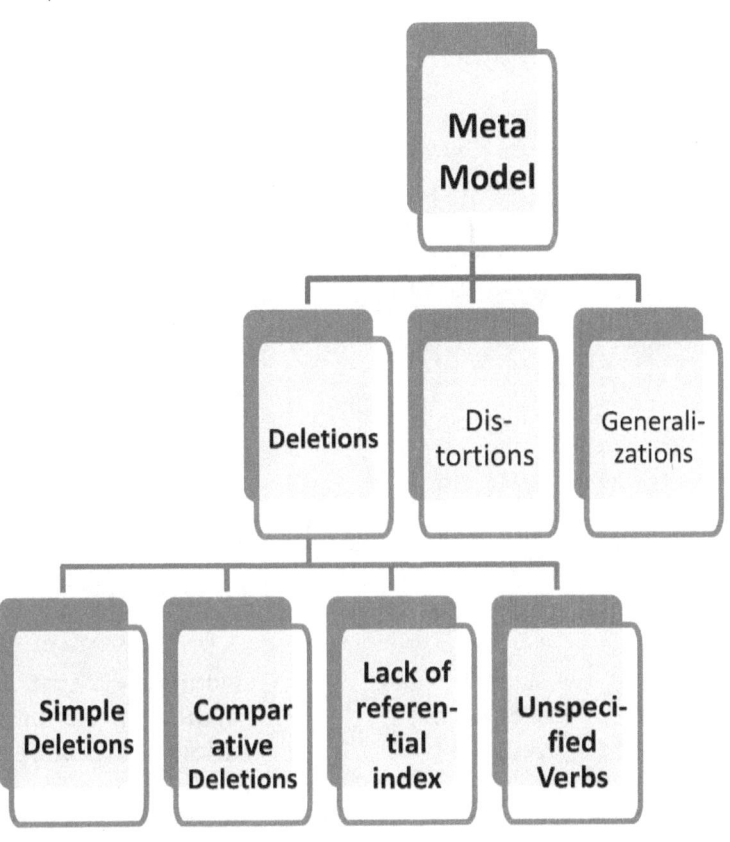

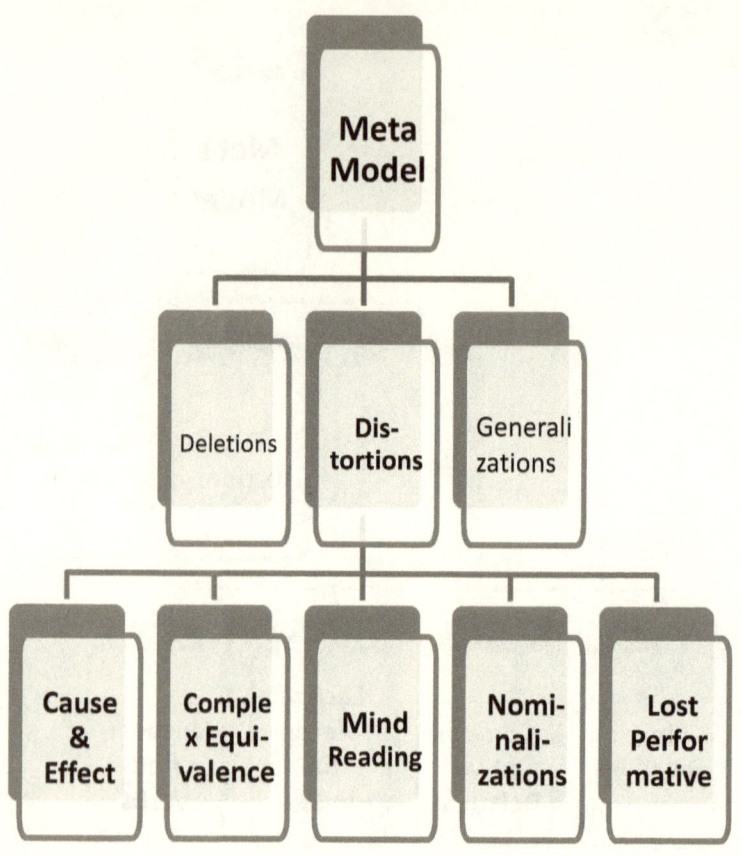

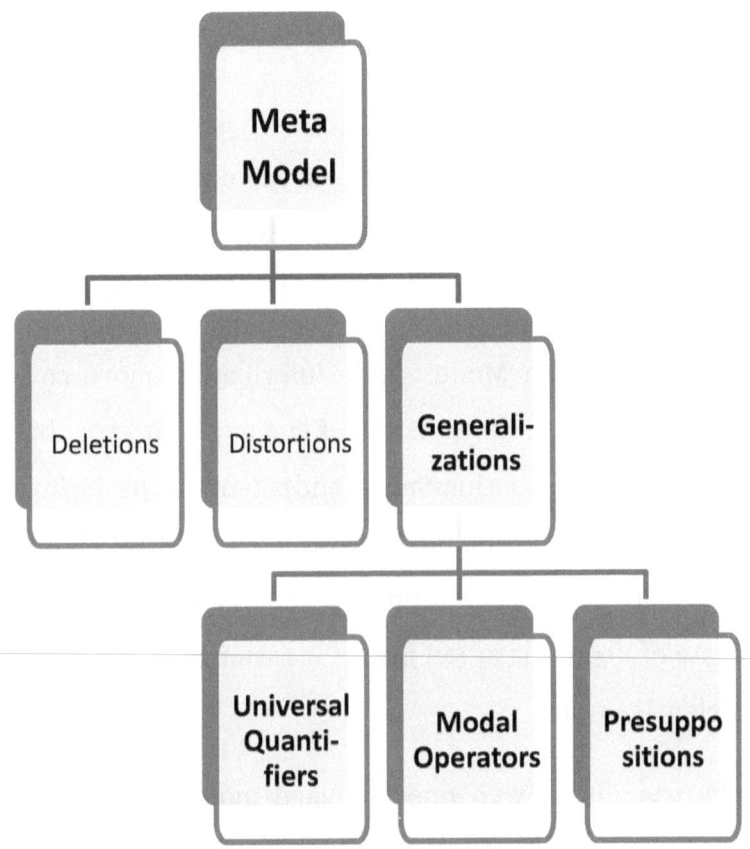

Clarifying vague information, however, is not the only thing that is needed to help people move forward in their growth process.

We've said it before: 'NLP deals with the language of the subconscious'.

It is the language with which we can outwit our resistances, our defense systems. And this language offers room for self-interpretation, for self-completion.

While the Meta Model made information more concrete, there is another model of language patterns that keeps the information vague and abstract: the **Milton Model**. The Milton Model is also used to bring people into a very deep relaxation, also called **trance**. And this state of deep relaxation makes it easier to break down defensive walls.

We can move from one language model to another, from detailed to global and vice versa, using '**chunking**':
- when you '**up chunk**', you ask questions about the bigger picture, you make things more global,
- when you '**down chunk**', you make things more detailed,
- when you '**lateral chunk**', you keep moving at the same level and get other information about the subject in question.

You can ask yourself: '**how do we get all of this done in concrete terms? How do we do this?**'

You will get an answer to these questions if you delve into the '**NLP Process for Change**'. This process describes the entire movement from where you are now to where you want to go and how this can be done. And here we start from the desired situation: 'What do you want?'

We are going to formulate **well-formed outcomes**, which must meet several criteria:

- **positively formulated and specific:**
    - it's about what you really want, not because you don't want to,
    - when you tell it, the other person should be able to experience the picture in his or her head.
- **personal:**
    - you have to own it,
    - you have to be able to send it yourself.
    Changing because someone else thinks you should do this doesn't work.

Relying on someone else's growth to achieve your own goal doesn't work either.

- **win-win for all (ecology):**
  - from your current situation, you take with you the things that you find good,
  - you are not causing harm to others, yourself, or society.
- **sensory testable:**
  - when do you know that you have reached your goal?
  - what will you see, hear, feel...?
  - what feedback from others do you need to get?

  You must have a sign somewhere that lets you know your goal has been accomplished.

Then we look at the **current situation**: 'How is it now?'

Here too we are going to ask some specific questions, including:

- what's your problem?
- how do you know it's a problem?
- what 'benefit' do you still get from it?

- what resources do you have available?

After that, we bridge the gap between the current situation and the desired situation, by using a series of **NLP techniques**.

Here we list some:
- rapport,
- eye signals,
- use of voice,
- language patterns,
- anchor,
- strategies,
- swish,
- timelines,
- visual squash,
- fast phobia cure,
- changing personal history,
- reframing.

The entire process is put together in a specific model: 'the **NLP Coaching Model**'.

This name may be misleading. It does not mean that it is only useful in the context of coaching. And it is equally applicable in other circumstances, in your daily life.

The **NLP Coaching Model** has a well-defined sequence:
- desired state,
- break state,
- current state,
- break state,
- applying techniques,
- break state,
- test,
- test future.

Note: there is NO break-state between the test and the test of the future!

And following that sequence is very important if you want to achieve the outcome you have in mind

Source: 'NLP™', Dr. Richard Bandler, Co-Founder of Neuro-Linguistic Programming
Source: Neuro-Linguïstisch Programmeren, de unieke handleiding voor jouw brein!, Alex Peeters & Marleen Devisch

The Barriers of Fear, the Terror Barrier

Whatever model we adopt, whatever our view on people, whatever we think about how a person is put together, when we take action, we all encounter the same thing: **'we run into barriers of fear, and we sabotage ourselves'**.

Thinking out dreams and desires is one thing. Turning them into action is another matter. And too many stop along the way because they don't feel like taking concrete steps again and again, because they feel afraid and can't overcome that fear, because they no longer believe they can because they are getting too far out of their comfort zone catapulted.

Taking action isn't always simple. We often function based on a lot of old habits and small rituals. And we are familiar with them. Changing and growing regularly means that we have to change those old habits, and we usually don't like that. We feel it pulling back. We recoil from that. And our initial enthusiasm subsides and in the end, everything stays the same.

What many don't know is that, once you understand what happens in such moments, it often takes just one push to get through them. If we manage to break through our fear wall, we are liberated and a whole new world of possibilities opens up.

We just need to learn to rely on this insight and learn to use the resources we have at our disposal. And all of this you can learn!

How does sabotage work?

The Barriers of Fear, the Terror Barrier...
Old beliefs, bad experiences...

We are often champions of sabotaging ourselves and our growth!

Vicious Sabotage Circle

                      Physical complaints

        Uncertainty   Emotional problems

Incomprehension   Social problems

          Conflicts   Social-cultural problems

                Relationship problems

We sabotage ourselves because we fear the unknown and because we want to protect ourselves from internal pain. Not wanting to feel pain, we choose safe, known paths and shrink from anything that deviates from them.

And only by continuing to take steps, through the fear, can we break through that self-sabotage.

Becoming aware of our self-sabotage mechanism is very important. For we can only do something with what we are aware of.

And doing nothing with that mechanism of sabotage means that our growth, or certain parts of it, remains inhibited or blocked to a greater or lesser extent.

If we are not aware of this system, we may be sending out double signals: something in us wants to grow and at the same time something else is holding us back. And we drive, as it were, with the handbrake on, we accelerate and brake at the same time, and we don't understand what keeps killing us.

What else can we do to prevent ourselves from getting stuck in self-sabotage?

Forgiveness

We could write a book only about 'forgiveness'!

Forgiveness is a process of letting go, bit by bit. Forgiveness doesn't happen all at once. It also doesn't happen by itself. It follows its path, often unnoticed, invisible. At a certain point, we feel that we have forgiven someone. We have stopped feeding our anger and/or hurt. When we meet the person we have forgiven, we no longer feel the painful charge in our feelings. And when we think of something for which we were angry with ourselves, we find that anger has been replaced by mildness.

'Forgiveness' does not happen with our mind, but with our heart. It is an internal event that cannot be imposed by anything or anyone. Truly forgiving is usually a 'silent' event. And we're not trumpeting it.

Stop Judging

We all judge. We are humans. Judging means that we put the other person in a box, often in an oversimplified way, without really knowing the other person or without checking whether our judgment is correct. And we stick a label. It's as if this makes us calmer. Often a judgment is a projection. We project our fear onto others and attribute all kinds of characteristics to it that we run away from. And we find someone bossy, stupid, irresponsible, and so on.

Often a judgment says more about us than about those we judge. After all, you cannot recognize in someone else what is not present in yourself either. Someone who is quick to accuse others of a breach of trust may not be very trustworthy himself. Someone who hates people with a different skin color will most likely have problems accepting certain aspects of their own identity or individuality. And we judge others because a similar judgment about ourselves would hurt us. And we wish to avoid that pain. So a judgment is a projection onto someone who is somehow a confrontational mirror to ourselves.

A judgment is different from an opinion. Judgments are colored by emotions, opinions are neutral. And we usually form an opinion basis on a different perception than a judgment. And an opinion starts from a different place in ourselves.

What to do with judgments?
1. accept the judgment. Don't judge yourself because you're passing judgment. It's human and you're learning,
2. being forgiving to yourself and others.

Break through the 'Barrier of Fear, the Terror Barrier'

Would you like to get out of your comfort zone?

Our 'comfort zone' is the safe feeling we have when we don't have too many new things coming our way. We live with known and predictable factors in and around us. There are a few challenges and that gives a certain peace of mind. However, this peace of mind is not growth-promoting in the long run, because if we only keep going on known paths, we will see little growth in our lives.

Growing by definition means getting out of our comfort zone because no growth can happen without changes. And to change you need to step out of your comfort zone!

Outside our comfort zone is fear, which makes us shrink back when we step outside that safe zone. Taking growth steps initially gives you a feeling of uncertainty. And we come out of our safe nest and that initially causes more or less 'fear of flying'. And if we keep going through this fear, we'll eventually find ourselves in much more pleasant waters. So perseverance is the message!

What can happen when you step out of your comfort zone?

The worst thing that can happen is that you grow, learn, gain new experiences. What is holding you back? Go for it! Do something that you don't dare to do and look at the result. And do something crazy and see what it causes in and around you. And learn from this!

Train yourself to step out of your comfort zone regularly

Think about the following. Getting out of your comfort zone regularly is a must if you want to grow as a person. Keeping moving is the key to keep moving internally. Thinking positively, with both feet on the ground, helps you to persevere. And keep going!

Following and making your dreams and desires come true is a wonderful thing to do. And you will of course also encounter obstacles on this path of growth.

Here are some more avenues that can help you deal with those obstacles:

Fear

Fear comes in many forms and degrees. It can express itself in various ways. And the basis of fear is usually a lack of insight or knowledge or a lack of self-confidence.

Solution: How do you handle this?

Fear very often has to do with too many unknown factors. And generally speaking, reducing fear means converting those unknown factors into known factors as much as possible.

If your fear is related to a lack of knowledge, you can keep up with that knowledge. Find out what knowledge you are missing, where you can acquire it, and what help you may need.

If you feel that you are lacking in insight, you can also ask for help or look for what you are missing now.

If your fear is related to a lack of self-confidence, learn to focus on your internal strength. Do everything you can to further develop that power. Focus on your abilities and develop them, deploy them in as many moments as possible. Focus on what you do have and what you can do, rather than on everything that isn't there in your life. And provide a life-giving environment in which you can be more and more yourself. Aim for a positive goal and take steps towards it every day. And get help if needed.

Keeping your goal in sight

If you want to achieve a goal, you need action. Just staring at the top of the mountain, where you so desperately want to be, is not enough. And you have to embark on the journey and start with the first step. The road to your goal is littered with many, often tempting, side roads. Don't get lost in all those sidetracks. And keep your focus on your target, like a compass always points north no matter where you are.

Several steps can provide you with planning and structure. On your way, you will also take many steps based on your intuition, without them belonging to a preconceived plan. Life brings all kinds of things. And every day is littered with invitations, with challenges, with opportunities to continue on your way. Daring to take steps without being sure whether it is the right step is an important part of your growth process.

Solution: How do you handle this?
Aim your 'compass', your focus, on your goal, and don't deviate from it. Make sure that your goal for yourself is clear and distinct, well-defined. And make a plan and at the same time leave space to let life do its work, space to follow your own intuition.

Your goal does not represent your real desire
It regularly happens that someone puts his or her goal into words, but after a while it turns out that there is another desire hidden under that goal. A goal expresses itself in a certain form. And a desire tells more about what is beneath that goal. It is the capacities within us that want to manifest, express themselves. And it could be that your goal is to make more money. That is a cer-

tain form. And it is quite possible that the desire that lies beneath this goal may be freedom.

It could just as well be that your goal is not yet clear, that you do not yet know what your goal actually is. And in this case, the way you have to go first is the way of finding a goal.

Solution: how do you handle this?

With every goal you have, ask yourself: 'What capacities of myself want to come out through this goal?'

For example: 'I want to travel the world' can mean your openness to different cultures, your eagerness to learn, your curiosity... want to grow. Or: 'I want a big house where I can receive a lot of people', can mean that the hospitality in you, your desire to be there for people, the social in you... want to come out. Focus mainly on those capacities and find the goal you can now move towards to shape them more.

Clarify your goal and make sure it is a reflection of your underlying desire to grow in certain aspects of yourself. What do you really want? Refine it, adjust it, grow in formulating it.

Use the strategies below to break through your 'Barrier of Fear, your Terror Barrier'

Set a goal that you can emotionally connect with
You have to hit a target. It should get you moving inside. Just thinking about your goal makes something flow within if it is your goal for now. And it keeps you very busy, you dream about it, you give a lot for it, it motivates you to take the necessary steps and overcome obstacles. Let your dream first find its way inside you. And enjoy.

Dare to take plenty of time to think about 'what it would be like if'. Dare to visualize your dream, your goal, and make it stronger in that way. And in the early stages, don't ask yourself how to do it all, because often this is the clincher that makes people say: 'it's not realistic, I can't do that, I don't dare, I can't, it's impossible...'.

And first, nurture your dream, nurture your motivation, become aware of much you want this, write down why you want this, and so on. And the steps required to achieve your goal flow from that, not vice versa.

Find out what you fear

Remember what you read about the comfort zone? Read it again if necessary! What happens inside you when you face a new challenge? What happens when there are changes in your life? When does your resistance start to work through fear, procrastination, restlessness, insecurity, excuses not to do something, lack of concentration, avoidance behavior, and so on?

We all have a 'zone' that is around our capabilities. A zone of fear and uncertainty. All kinds of defense mechanisms, which like faithful soldiers watch over that our lives remain as it is. And it is a part of us that is responsible for the stability in our existence. Stability in itself is important, of course, but not if it holds back our growth.

And defense systems want to stop us from growing, want to keep us in the safety of our comfort zone, want to protect us from all kinds of 'dangers'. And they have been installed in us at some point, for whatever reason.

But now they are often just an obstacle that slows our growth or stops it.

Understanding how these mechanisms work is enormous wealth. And the better we learn to deal with it, the stronger we are to continue growing and to continue to embark on a journey outside our comfort zone.

Steps, steps, steps...

Keep walking. Even if you advance millimeter by millimeter, it doesn't matter, as long as you keep moving. Enjoy the road in itself. Often people think that they will not be happy until they reach their goal. Nothing could be further from the truth.

And the road to the goal is littered with life, with oxygen, with the intensity of life, with enjoying the growth and development you go through. With every step you take, you become more human, more yourself, more than authentic person that is hidden inside you. And feeling this gives people a boost of energy.

And in the long run, this train will no longer be stopped. You also don't want her to stop. You increasingly feel the obstacles you encounter as learning experiences. And you develop the strength to deal with them and to turn them into sources of power that make you stronger.

Out of Your Comfort Zone? Build a party!
Aborigines, the original inhabitants of Australia, do not celebrate birthdays. They celebrate growth. Every time someone from the tribe thinks that he or she has grown into something, a party is thrown. And you initially recognize growth by the fear, unrest, insecurity... that you feel because you are being pulled out of your comfort zone.

And this should be the signal to throw a party, for it is the beginning of something new, the announcement of the 'birth' of new life that is finding its way out within you.

And when you focus on that new life, on the capacities within you that are trying to find their way out, you get a very different story than when you focus on your fear. Even if you are a helper of people or responsible for a group, for example, it can help if people have fear, to direct them to the power in them that wants to manifest itself.

Repeat is the key!
It doesn't happen by itself. Growing demands an effort, a commitment. It takes commitment and perseverance. And the road to your goal is not always easy. Sometimes you may wonder why, what you are doing, whether it makes sense, and so on. At those moments it is very important to fall back on a strong motivation.

In addition, working every day with your goal is a must. Continuing to repeat where you want to go, why you want it, and the steps you're about to take is the key to actually achieving your goal. And practice makes perfect, absolutely applies here!

Repetition also applies when you have reached a goal and are looking for a new goal. Continuing to set goals, keep challenging yourself and get out of your comfort zone, overcoming that fear time and again, gives your life meaning and keeps you energetic and happy.

And all this does not mean that there should be no rest breaks in your life, quite the contrary. Taking a break in your comfort zone can allow you to recharge your batteries and then get back on the road. Only when you feel that you are no longer growing, the time has come to give yourself another push from that safe nest...

Afterword

You have reached the end of this book. Hopefully, you have learned a lot from it, and you will take the tools we have provided you with on your growth path.

This book is intended as a dynamic whole. And what's in it grew out of years of research and experience working with people. It's not finished. It may grow further and be enriched with new or even more in-depth content. And everything and everyone is in constant growth and evolution. So is this book.

Integrate what you have read and use it in a personal way. Don't just take everything blindly. Think for yourself. And take what interests you and what helps you. And let go of what is not for now or where you don't feel a connection with. Get on the road and experience whether it really helps you.

If you have suggestions to make this book better, we'd love to hear them. Because the story can be written further...

If you have any questions, if you need help, please contact us. We are happy to help you further on your way!

And we wish you a lot of growth!

Alex Peeters & Marleen Devisch

Licensed Trainers of Neuro-Linguistic Programming®
Licensed Coaching Trainers of Neuro-Linguistic Programming®

References

Books

- '100 en gezond' - John Robbins
- '7 lessen in emotionele intelligentie' - Patrick E. Merlevede & Rudy C. Vandamme
- 'As A Man Thinketh' - James Allen
- 'Bevrijd jezelf: Met EFT naar meer evenwicht in le leven' - Koen Van Reeth & Veronique Schelfaut
- 'Coach jezelf naar succes' - Talane Miedaner
- 'Coaching' - Bram Gerrits
- 'Creatief visualiseren' - Shakti Gawain
- 'Creëer je eigen toekomst' - Eddy van der Wereld
- 'De kracht van angst - Van machteloos naar moeiteloos' - Eddie van der Wereld en Marc Schwencke
- 'De kracht van verandering' - Dr. Wayne W. Dyer
- 'De Oorsprong van The Secret' - Wallace D. Wattles & Bart van den Hoogen
- 'De praktijk van het genieten' - Wilfried Van Craen
- 'De Rijkdom van de Law of Attraction' - Esther & Jerry Hicks
- 'De Sleutel' - Joe Vitale
- 'De sleutels tot succes' - Napoleon Hill
- 'De zeven spirituele wetten van succes' - Deepak Chopra
- 'De wet van de verbindingskracht' - Michael Losier
- 'Denk groot en word rijk' - Napoleon Hill
- 'Dit boek moet je hebben om te bereiken wat je wilt' - Mark Palmer & Scott Solder

- 'FLOW. Psychologie van de optimale ervaring.' - Mihaly Csikszentmihalyi
- 'Gebruik je verstand' - Tony Buzan
- 'Haal het beste uit uw persoonlijkheid' - Lothar Seiwert & Friedbert Gay
- 'Handleiding voor het leven' - Joe Vitale
- 'Het handboek voor Coaching - Deel I: Coaching Basics' - Life University
- 'Het handboek voor Coaching - Deel II : Mental Coaching' - Life University
- 'Het handboek voor Coaching - Deel III : Transformational Coaching' - Life University
- 'Het kleine boek van de creativiteit' - George Parker
- 'Het miljonairsbrein ontrafeld' - T. Harv Eker
- 'Het Secret Dankbaarheidsboek' - Rhonda Byrne
- 'Hulp uit het universum' - Jonathan Cainer
- 'Hoe overleef ik mijn collega's?' - Jan Yager
- 'Je bent rijk geboren' - Bob Proctor, 2007
- 'Je kunt je leven helen' - Louise L. Hay
- 'Je ongekende vermogens' - Anthony Robbins
- 'Je wordt wat je denkt' - Inge Rock
- 'Leef volgens de wet van de aantrekkingskracht' - Jack Canfield & Watkins, D.D.
- 'Lessen in levenskunst' - Wilfried Van Craen
- 'Lessen in levenskunst' - Dr. Wayne W. Dyer
- 'Lichaamstaal voor Dummies' - Elizabeth Kuhnke
- 'Life Coaching voor Dummies' - Jeni Mumford

- 'Life planning, de ontbrekende schakel tussen geld en gevoel', George Kinder, Uitgeverij: Rozhanitsa, 2009
- 'Loslaten' - Jan Wolter Bijleveld & Ingeborg Deana
- 'Loslaten en leren vertrouwen' - Susanne Hühn
- 'Mentor van nu' - Klaas Jan Terpstra & Herberd Prinsen, 2010
- 'Mijn ziel mijn zaligheid' - Dr. Wayne W. Dyer
- 'Naar het hart van communicatie' - Eric Schneider
- 'NLP voor Dummies' - Romilla Ready & Kate Burton
- 'Overtuigen - Een kunst die je kunt leren!' - Hans Christian Altmann
- 'Psychometrische tests' - Philip Carter & Ken Russell
- 'Quantum-Touch' - Richard Gordon
- 'Prettig gestoord - Bizarre kronkels bij gewone mensen' - Wilfried Van Craen
- 'Relaxatie en zelfhypnose in de praktijk' - Wilfried Van Craen
- 'Sleutels tot positief denken' - Napoleon Hill en Michael J. Ritt Jr.
- 'Stop! Geen excuses meer' - Dr. Wayne W. Dyer
- 'Succes door een positieve instelling' - Napoleon Hill & W. Clement Stone
- 'The Attractor Factor' - Joe Vitale
- 'The Really Good Fun Cartoon Book of NLP' - Philip Miller
- 'The Power' - Rhonda Byrne
- 'The Secret' - Rhonda Byrne
- 'The secret of The Secret' - Karen Kelly
- 'Trainingsboek zelfvertrouwen - Je eigen grenzen overwinnen' - Rob Vellekoop
- 'Transformerend coachen' - Chérie Carter-Scott
- 'Uw geheugen de baas' - Tony Buzan

- 'Verander je leven met NLP' - David Molden & Path Hutchinson
- 'Visuele waarneming: de psychologie van het zien' - R. L. Gregory
- 'Voor hetzelfde geld rijk' - Joop korthuis
- 'Waar blijft mijn bestelling toch?!' - Bärbel Mohr
- 'Werkboek Visualiseren' - Ko Vos & Fransje de Jongh
- 'Wie ben je echt!' - Roy Martina

Audiobooks

- '144 Strategies for Success and Happiness' - Andrew Matthews
- 'Clearing Your internal Obstacles To Success' - Bob Proctor, Jack Canfield, Tony Robbins, ...
- 'De groeimoter - Innovatie van markten en merken' - Roland en Rogier van Krakelingen
- 'I Can Do It' - Louise L. Hay
- 'Nieuwe producten bedenken - De effectieve VOORT-methode.' - Gijs van Wulfen
- 'Receiving Prosperity' - Louise L. Hay
- 'Self Esteem Affirmations' - Louise L. Hay
- 'The American Monk Prosperity Program' - Burt Goldman
- 'The Attractor Factor' - Joe Vitale
- 'The Magic of Thinking Big' - David J. Schwartz
- 'The Missing Secret' - Joe Vitale
- 'The Secret of Imagining' - Neville Goddard
- 'You Can Heal Your Life' - Louise L. Hay
- 'Zero Limits' - Joe Vitale

NLP Communication Institute

Training Institute and Expertise Center for NLP
licensed by the Society of NLP™

GROEI ACADEMIE BV

Katelijnestraat 116a
8000 BRUGGE

GSM
+32 50 94 68 43

E-Mail
info@groeiacademie.be

The Society of NLP™

GROEI ACADEMIE BV is affiliated with the international Society of Neuro Linguistic Programming™

GROEI ACADEMIE BV is recognized as an **NLP Training Institute in Belgium** by the international Society of Neuro Linguistic Programming™.

Alex Peeters and **Marleen Devisch** can be found both as **Licensed Trainer of NLP™** and as **Licensed Coaching Trainer of NLP™** in Database of Licensed Trainers of Neuro-Linguistic Programming™.

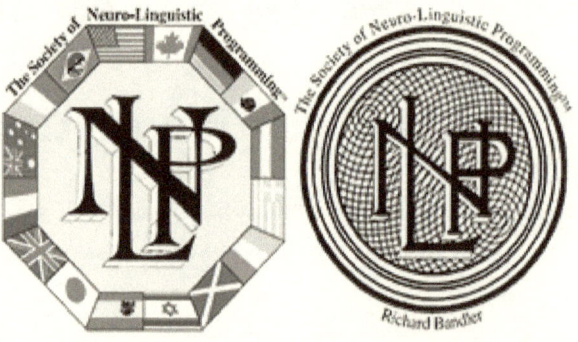

The Society of NLP™ founded by **Dr. Richard Bandler** in 1978, is the oldest and worldwide largest organization for NLP. It was founded for the purpose of exercising quality control over training programs and services representing the model of Neuro-Linguistic Programming (NLP™).

Dr. Richard Bandler and **John La Valle**, supported by **Kathleen La Valle**, are actively developing NLP and training new NLP Practitioners, NLP Master Practitioners, NLP Advanced Master Practitioners, NLP Trainers, NLP Coaching Trainers, ... The way Dr. Richard Bandler teaches NLP has evolved over the years to 'the simpler, the better'.

NLP Communication Institute

GROEI ACADEMIE, the NLP Communication Institute par excellence, with the most complete offer within Europe!

We teach how to use your brain, change your life, so that more energy and life dynamics are released, and you experience more happiness and successful acting!

Those who train with us choose trainers with a great deal of experience who teach you, "to 'Think' differently, to 'Communicate' differently to Influence with Impact, for a life with **Maximum Quality of Life & Success** in all areas of life!"

Our starting point is: "Every human being has a **'diamond'** in himself! Some are already partly polished, others are still quite rough. At GROEI ACADEMIE we provide an **NLP toolbox**, so that you can polish this diamond yourself, up to your desired level: beginner, advanced, advanced to expert!"

At GROEI ACADEMIE, we do what we do because we believe that everyone deserves Maximum Quality of Life and Success! We put our focus on the strengths and opportunities in people's differences, not their limitations. And we live what we teach to others. This is also our aspiration in all our trainings: "that what people learn there becomes a life attitude, your way of being."

The participants who find the greatest satisfaction with us are those who want a full-fledged NLP toolbox and who intend to go through the various levels from beginners, advanced, advanced to experts, with this toolbox. They do this in order to eventually become true experts in it, greatly enhancing and accelerating their professional & personal growth, making them much more effective, and with impact communicating & influencing, training, coaching, motivating, speaking to lifting themselves to another dimension!

Our NLP trainings include the levels: 'Practitioner, Master, Coach & Advanced', also the Business-levels. They are internationally recognized NLP trainings and courses by the 'Society of NLP™'. We train from experience: <u>no theory or talking about</u>, but <u>a lot of doing</u>, from the lived **CODEC model**!

So grant you our powerful **NLP toolbox** usable <u>in the Workplace</u>, <u>in Daily Life</u>, in <u>Communication with people with autism and their environment.</u>

The Power of Our Thinking!

Living from your authentic power

We all think. We process millions of stimuli every day, which come to us from outside. We filter the information coming in. It connects with pre-existing memories, thinking patterns... And we go to work with that to build our world, to respond to others, to behave in any way.

Have you ever thought about what could change in your life if you were able to control a large part of your thinking? To be able to stop worrying if you want to? To keep you in the mood you want? To say constructive things to yourself in the face of adversity instead of screwing yourself up?

By learning to 'play' with what is going on in your head, you create infinite more possibilities for yourself to lead a happier life.

Alex Peeters & **Marleen Devisch**

The Power of Our Thinking!

Living from your authentic power

We all think. We process millions of stimuli every day, which come to us from outside. We filter the information coming in. It connects with pre-existing memories, thinking patterns... And we go to work with that to build our world, to respond to others, to behave in any way.

Have you ever thought about what could change in your life if you were able to control a large part of your thinking? To be able to stop worrying if you want to? To keep you in the mood you want? To say constructive things to yourself in the face of adversity instead of screwing yourself up?

By learning to 'play' with what is going on in your head, you create infinite more possibilities for yourself to lead a happier life.

Alex Peeters & Marleen Devisch

www.ingramcontent.com/pod-product-compliance
Lightning Source LLC
Chambersburg PA
CBHW030449220526
45464CB00006B/2453